CONTENTS

IMPERFECT HEALING

A MEDITATION ON BEGINNING
AGAIN IN AMERICA

Noah Micah Dorson

Copyright 2022

"If, with mindfulness' rope,
The elephant of the mind is tethered all around,
Our fears will come to nothing,
Every virtue drop into our hands."

Shantideva, *The Way of the Bodhisattva*

Dedication

This book is dedicated to my father, Mitch. May this book continue your legacy of joyfulness, enthusiasm, and kindness. I love you.

I also dedicate this book to Steven Weygint for your patient contributions to the editing process. As a new writer, I could never have finished this project without your love, support, and expertise. With all my heart, thank you.

TABLE OF CONTENTS

Appendix: Buddhist Meditation Peer Recovery Script and Meeting

Author's Note

The teachings in this book build upon the writings of Buddhist nun and author, Pema Chodron, along with Buddhist teachers and authors Sharon Salzberg and Jack Kornfield. All three of these extraordinary people have studied and practiced extensively with renowned meditation scholars and teachers all over the world. Pema Chodron, Sharon Salzberg, and Jack Kornfield continue to write and teach in a way that works with, rather than against, our fast-paced American lives. The content and meditations that touch upon the Buddhist traditions of basic goodness, lovingkindness, and tonglen ("taking and sending") come from my personal study of their teachings.

In composing this book, I have been guided primarily by Pema Chodron's *Start Where You Are-A Guide to Compassionate Living; When Things Fall Apart-Heart Advice for Difficult Times; The Places That Scare You-A Guide to Fearlessness in Difficult Times;* Sharon Salzberg's *Lovingkindness-The Revolutionary Art of Happiness;* and Jack Kornfield's *A Path with Heart-The Perils and Promises of Spiritual Life.* These books have been life sustaining for me and countless others pursuing a spiritual path in America today.

In addition, the teachings from His Holiness the

Dalai Lama on "altruism and interdependence" make up an important part of this book. *The Wisdom of Forgiveness-Intimate Conversations and Journeys,* written by the Dalai Lama and Victor Chan, has also had a tremendous impact on my own writing style, understanding of Buddhist traditions, and daily life. With sincere gratitude, I want to thank all four of these amazing teachers for their guidance and tremendous endeavors in the name of mindfulness and healing.

A Beginning: Mental Health and
Imperfect Healing in America

"We must accept finite disappointment, but never lose infinite hope."
Dr. Martin Luther King, Jr.

Mental health and mental illness have historically been red-flagged terms in our country. This is especially true when people who are familiar and even intimate with the challenges of mental health bring it up. If such discussions do arise, we tend to shut them down or sidestep them as quickly as possible. In tough times when we experience isolation, grief, or confusion, it can be extremely uncomfortable to discuss our own mental health and how we cope with fear, addiction, and loneliness. Rather than opening and sharing our internal lives with others, we tend to push away our feelings out of embarrassment and carry on as though everything is fine.

However, from experience with mindfulness practice and my invaluable time within a Community of Recovery, I now understand that this is not the compassionate way to address mental health or mental illness in our country. Although we might turn away from these uncomfortable exchanges on mental health, courageous leaders all over America are carving out spaces where thousands, if not millions of people, can experience their vulnerability and tenderness to grow stronger physically, emotionally, and spiritually. These leaders, appearing in various positions of service throughout the nation, have become our real-life heroes at a time when we are calling out for authentic, strong, and compassionate leadership.

Through the composition of this book, I have been privileged to share my experience with being part of a Recovery Community and my own process of maturation and emotional healing during that critical time in my life. Furthermore, the conception of this book, *Imperfect Healing*, has been a wonderful and thought-provoking exercise in the exploration of meditation and how spiritual practice may benefit not just a handful, but an immeasurable number of people all over the country.

Beginning my own spiritual journey of imperfect healing, as we will call it throughout these chapters, I had to stop and breathe with mindfulness multiple times each day. Practicing slowly and with purpose, I started to focus on feeling my body from within and relaxing through old layers of built-up tension. This experience of mindfulness, the act of breathing and slowing down, eventually led me to stop worrying so much about the future and stay more in the present moment. Even if it was only for five minutes a day, by taking the time to inhale and exhale with gentleness, I discovered that I was doing myself and everyone around me a great service in the spirit of self-care, tending to emotional wounds that I had left unchecked for a long time. Whether it was stopping to look up at the open blue sky or breathe in the scent of fresh flowers, by practicing mindfulness I found my way back to the small moments of life that made me feel alive and well once more.

As people read my story, it is my deepest hope that you will find a moment or two to slow down, step back, and breathe mindfully yourself. Although it may seem like a simple task, one that we can put aside and pick up again when we have more time, I have found the opposite to be true. Finding space to breathe and cultivate mindfulness each day will not only help us create a bit of distance from our busy schedules, but also uncover a tender connection to the people in our lives. With time, we will find that this sense of connection is the very root of healing and joy that we can tap into at any time and in any place.

As we journey together through these chapters, I also hope that we may find daily opportunities to remember how precious we are and how precious this world is. Regardless of which faith or spiritual practice we identify with, I aspire that this simple book can serve as an additional resource to anyone wishing to reemerge from a difficult past into a life filled with wonder, possibility, and even enthusiasm for the future. Walking this imperfect path as friends, may we discover that there is still ample time to breathe, let go, and unearth our basic joy and kindness at this very moment, wherever we may find ourselves.

CHAPTER 1: IMPERFECT AND PERFECT

"Each of you is perfect the way you are...and you could use a little improvement!"

Suzuki Roshi-Zen Teacher and Master

I am not *"perfect,"* at least not in terms of modern-day standards and perceptions of perfection. My body, no matter the hundreds of sit-ups and push-ups I do, will not be on the cover of *GQ* or *Esquire Magazine.* My mind, possessing a basic and admirable intelligence, is not destined for a Rhodes Scholarship! At first, embracing these facts-of-life can be embarrassing and challenging to do. "If only I was smarter and if only my body was more naturally beautiful, everything would be perfect," was a common theme in my thinking growing up. While I have tried to shy away from those that I love without the safety net of these perfections, my "imperfections" of emotional sensitivity, burning dedication, and passion for cultivating a tender heart can inspire that redemptive spark of goodness, which makes this life worth living to the fullest.

From the moment my eyes open until it is time for sleep, this imperfect mind and body is striving and even struggling to comprehend the unfolding of life's events. As we all know too well, control is an unfair and finite commodity often just outside of our reach, even if we deserve a little more of it. Still, like so many brave spiritual explorers on the road during these chaotic times, I am resilient, simmering with a steady and tender courage. Hopefully not too proud, this courage tethers itself to a quiet confidence and a bit of humility. It can shine through in the expression of gratitude for having dependable people in my life, spontaneous and inappropriate laughter, and five conscious breaths before becoming overwhelmed.

Truly, all of us have had moments of fearlessness when we are unfazed by the passing storms of pleasant and not so pleasant thoughts and feelings. Even with the daily imperfections of struggling to find a 9-5, stubbing a toe for the tenth time on a nearby table, or waking up at 5am to the loud "Chirp!" of a dead fire-alarm battery, we can still find a tiny flickering flash of happiness that glows and hums on inside of us. While I realize that I am far from perfect, particularly when things fall apart and do not go to plan, I am mindful that this life is a tremendous gift and that I would not change it for anything, even if I could. Not only am I grateful and blessed to have this one precious life, as often discussed in the Buddhist tradition, but I am willing to take the next best step along this unknown journey of twenty-four hours.

Even so, sometimes the cracks in the concrete open, taking back this sense of wisdom and courage that I once possessed. This has been my experience in the past when I begin a new job or move to a new place. Whether I am tending to late night folks at a restaurant, trying to teach seventh graders about American Civics, or seeing the sunset for the first time in our new Texas hometown, the experience is so fresh and immediate that I find it difficult to be present in the moment. Every new experience in a new space has the potential to become overwhelming, leaving my heart in spiritual "no-man's land," as defined by Buddhist teacher Pema Chodron.

Stepping into this unfamiliar territory, whether it is inside or out, exposes dimensions of bravery and a couple that I would rather keep hidden and safe.

As people read this passage, hopefully you can empathize with the process of stepping into the spiritual wilderness of groundlessness and not knowing what will happen next. If you are familiar with this kind of curious occurrence, it might be interesting to ask: "What does this shift feel like in my body?" and "How do I meet such change and uncertainty with compassion and courage?" If you can, take three minutes before reading any further to reflect on how you responded to a minute or substantial change in your own life and what you may have learned from it.

Like myself, most people reading this book may be amazed and even humbled by our ever-shifting reactions to daily events and emotions. If we take a big step back and observe ourselves from a distance, we can even bear witness to our state of mind moving back and forth between happiness, sorrow, irritation, tenderness, sleepiness, inspiration, and somehow back to happiness once again! Seeing this chain reaction of internal responses, we could then explore how each moment holds the potential to uncover our strength, flexibility, and vulnerability as human beings.

This basic human dilemma appeared in my own life not so long ago in the summer of 2022. On a hot afternoon in Denton, Texas shortly after moving from Seattle, Washington my life-partner, Zim, and I decided to drive all around town running errands and getting acquainted with our new community. Throughout the course of our journeys, we quickly found ourselves in conversation about politics and its impact on American families, then laughing at random magazine covers, then reflecting nostalgically about our dads, then eating lunch, and finally finding time to go grocery shopping. Zim and I filled up the day with our own style of banter and jubilation, as though we were two kids given permission to gallivant and fly all about, causing just a little bit of trouble in our new hometown.

When we got home to our extended-stay hotel, I took our dog, Gizmo, out for a sweltering walk in the sun. During the month of June in North Central Texas, when temperatures can climb to one-hundred degrees plus, it is a blessing to step into any air-conditioned space and I immediately felt grateful to get my panting doggo out of danger from passing out. As Gizmo and I returned to our hotel room and started hydrating, Zim walked into the kitchen, took one look at me, and bellowed, "Oh my God! What happened to your pants?" Looking down at my backside (Gizmo may have peaked, as well), I quickly discovered a greasy kitchen-looking stain on my blue shorts that Zim had bought for me. "How could you do this... again?" he exclaimed in frustration. Unnerved and embarrassed, I responded, "It was not intentional, I promise! But do not worry, honey, it will come out." "No, it won't!" Zim exclaimed! "Yes, it will! Of course, it will!" I pleaded. Thus, it went for the next thirty minutes, back and forth, up, down, and around the bend until we both settled down and allowed cooler heads to prevail. Looking back, what had been an adventurous day filled with laughter and future tripping, rapidly fell apart into a disagreement surrounding my lifelong struggle to keep clothes clean and indeed, in one piece!

This experience, while nothing extraordinary or unusual for couples, I hope, shows the perfect and imperfect nature of being alive, complete with the exhilaration of companionship and the embarrassment of screwing it all up. Like that day in Denton, which I will call the "The Nearly Perfect Day," we as a species experience so much, deriving such intimate meaning in our daily experiences instantaneously. Our understanding of the world at once joyous, is also fragile, something that we cannot quite capture in these few pages.

While we may have inherited struggles and fears from the past, our strength and compassion carry-on, like my husband and I did after The Nearly Perfect Day. Though we may wish to be "better than the next person" and find uninterrupted external comfort, it is from our challenges that we may gain insight into what it means to be healthy and whole despite our imperfections. The practice of accepting and getting to know our worries and fears, pleasures and ideals, and times both wonderful and bewildering have led to the possibility of drafting this book and exploring the nature of healing, an imperfect healing, as we will define for ourselves throughout this journey together.

Moving from chapter to chapter, it remains a fervent hope that this exploration of imperfect healing can refresh our resolve to swim with the waves of life. Outside of this book alone, it is this image of swimming and finding our own way through the waters that I pray inspires us to stay inquisitive and inspired, even when things get tough. As someone who is always learning to ride these waves more skillfully, I am immensely grateful for having this opportunity to share my story and learn how to swim just a little bit better as a result.

With all my heart, thank you again for coming along with me on this personal exploration. Although it has been challenging to articulate my story concisely and coherently at times, I have written freely, unencumbered by fear or doubt. I remain humbled and in awe to put into words what imperfect healing means to me and why it matters so much in America today. Again, thank you for making this dream of sharing my story into a reality. It could not have been possible without you and your gracious encouragement.

Taking a beat before moving on, I would like to pose a couple of questions that might help us remain open and even curious along this journey of imperfect healing:

1. **How do we rediscover ourselves, our better selves, after challenging times?**
2. **What are the pathways that may help us reconnect, reintegrate, reenergize, and better love the people and the world around us?**
3. **Wherever we are, how do we forgive and begin again, trusting in our own basic-goodness and tender heart?**

These questions are challenging to ask, even during good times. Still, it my hope that we take these questions personally as we explore the process of healing, imperfect as it may be.

CHAPTER 2: FINDING A PLACE IN THE ROOMS OF RECOVERY

"God, grant me the serenity to the accept the things I cannot change, courage to change the things I can, and the wisdom to know the difference."
Reinhold Neibuhr, *Serenity Prayer*

Around my twenty-fifth birthday, I started opening and sharing about my struggles as a young man seeking to develop a spiritual practice to address concerns around mental health and mental well-being. Since graduating from college, I had kept myself busy with finding and maintaining work in the service industry and politics at the state and national level. While I quite enjoyed the work in both departments, I also discovered that I had less and less time to step back and reflect on the choices I was making personally and professionally. My time was becoming so stretched in fact that I no longer questioned whether the direction of my life was sustainable and if this was the right path for me to be on.

At the end 2008, coming off more than a year of campaigning for a candidate at the highest level of office, I found myself in a state of physical and emotional exhaustion, completely burned out. Although the wild ride of the campaign was an amazing experience, filled with wonderful, supportive, and enthusiastic people from all over the country, I would be fortunate to get off the rollercoaster of working twelve-hour days and sleeping only four to five hours a night. Following the stress and excitement of Election Night after all the votes were in, I was ready to go home and slowly step away from a job associated with American politics. Money, thankfully, was not an issue at the time and I was able to reconsider what I needed most to get my health, energy, and even sanity back. In hindsight, eventually walking away from a career in politics was one of the best decisions I ever made.

Returning home to Seattle, I found support groups and open recovery meetings in my community where I could sit and listen to the stories of countless people moving through tremendous personal adversities. Whether it was recovery from past trauma or substance abuse, I would see that those who attended meetings were also embracing sobriety and cultivating a foundation for mental and spiritual well-being. Under the supportive umbrella of this Recovery Community back home in the Capitol Hill Neighborhood, I started to sense as though something transformational could happen for me as well.

After an intense year straight of political campaigning, it was an extraordinary thing to find open and welcoming places where I could witness people coming together and being emotionally accessible to one another, in good times and in not such good times. In the world of recovery, whether it was from substance abuse, sex and romantic relationships, or even old childhood fears, I experienced the meaning of being compassionately mindful and present. "Old timers," people with years of sobriety under their belt, would display grit and compassion by offering their gradual process of getting clean and staying sober. At the same time, these Old Timers would leave space for newcomers to express their confusion and frustration with the slow and typically painstaking process of recovery from addiction.

Taking the time to welcome a newcomer, regardless of who they were or where they came from, was the medicine that my fellows freely gave away to help each other become stronger in their recovery from addiction. Whether it was taking someone out for a cup of coffee after a meeting, offering a bright smile to someone looking down and afraid, or even cooking breakfast for a friend who needed a little extra company, I kept seeing people take positive action for their fellows, and in doing so, grow more confident spiritually and in their sobriety.

I will never forget after one early morning meeting taking the time to cook oatmeal for a new fellow diagnosed with HIV and struggling to get clean without proper housing. He was tired and a little shaken up, but also grateful for the chance to be in community with those who related to his experience of trying to get sober under exceedingly difficult conditions. As we cooked our oatmeal on the stovetop and talked about our plans for the day ahead, I could see on his face that the morning fellowship had touched his heart deeply, giving him just a little more strength to keep going and not give up.

As time passed, I would witness this same friend attending meetings and slowly cultivating a recovery support system to help him get clean and stay sober. Little by little, my friend would start to put the pieces of his life back together by placing recovery at the forefront of his world and rebuilding trust that things could and would turn around for him. Thankfully, he would find stable housing and even enter a job training program to serve as a drug rehabilitation counselor in the community. Working in such a position, my friend would eventually be able to support countless people in the process of getting clean themselves, drawing from his own personal experience to help guide those along their strenuous and hopefully exhilarating journeys.

Thinking back on this fellow's courageous story, I feel heartened and deeply encouraged. His journey and experiences are living proof that such healing, imperfect and challenging as it may be, is possible when people have a place to come together, lift each other up, and be of service! Those who may seem damaged and beyond repair at first sight are not beyond redemption. On the contrary, with time, diligent work, and care, people new to recovery can heal and become renewed in mind, body, and spirit. Truly we can rise from the ashes of addiction and pain stronger and more vibrant than we could ever have imagined.

This shared experience of healing and connection is nothing new, but an ancient tradition that spans back to the origins of Tibetan Buddhism. In the Dalai Lama's book, coauthored with Victor Chan, *The Wisdom of Forgiveness: Intimate Conversations and Journeys,* they describe the significant importance of "altruism and interdependence" to lead a happy and fulfilling life. Altruism, according to the Dalai Lama, is the willingness to think of others and care for them deeply. Like my fellows in The Rooms of Recovery, who were taking newcomers under their wing, they too were practicing altruism at an everyday "kitchen sink level," as Pema Chodron often says. The teachings on altruism from the Dalai Lama and countless people in recovery was simple, yet profound: every act and thought are significant, no matter how small.

We see altruism of this kind in the well-known

parable about a grandfather and grandson walking along an oceanfront. After strolling a while down their path, both men would discover the beach before them littered with washed up starfish drying out along the sandy shore. The story goes that when the grandfather saw the shoreline filled with dying starfish, he immediately started tossing them back into the ocean one at a time. When his grandson saw this, he shouted to his grandfather, "There are too many. You could never save them all! Why does it matter?" Throwing yet one more starfish back into the ocean, the grandfather turned to his grandson and said, "It meant something to that one."

In the Rooms of Recovery, it was quite extraordinary to witness people take on leadership roles of sponsorship and service, paving the way for healing and renewal like the grandfather did in the parable. Reaching out with helping hands to newcomers, leaders in the community would mentor and model the formidable potential of living life in sobriety. People who had at one time experienced isolation because of their addiction would now lead the way for those like myself, searching for a community and a lifeline to something sustainable and sacred. During this critical time in recovery, I witnessed what healing looks like in action. After years in the cycle of addiction, these courageous men and women would slowly find their way back to sanity by working their program of recovery and being of benefit and service to their fellows.

In addition to their altruistic action, those in our Recovery Community would take time every day to pray and meditate. In time, I would follow their example by becoming more conscious of my breathing during meetings. Day after day, I would sit, breathe, and listen to people share their extraordinary journeys, soaking up each moment like a child returned to their mother after a long separation. In retrospect, this precious time would become my introduction to mindful meditation and a profound reminder of what it means to be "basically good," according to Buddhist tradition.

Connected to altruism, "interdependence" refers to how our thoughts and actions may have an immediate, lasting, and even cumulative impact on ourselves and the lives of others. The Dalai Lama teaches that by learning about interdependence we may fundamentally understand that what we do on a day-to-day basis is of great significance. He goes further by explaining that our actions will not just benefit those we know intimately, but potentially the community we live in, our hometown, state, country, and even the entire world.

Reflecting on the teachings found in the "starfish parable," interdependence shows us that even if we cannot help every person we meet, we might be able to inspire others to engage and lend a helping hand. In the spirit of healing and taking ownership of this precious world, each of us may have a part to play. Like the grandson on the ocean shore, we too can take positive action by tapping into the courage of our hearts, a little bit at a time. Fundamentally, it will take profound courage to be there for others when circumstances seem out of control. Sometimes, when we find ourselves confused or angry at the very people we wish to help, it may seem like an impossible task to be kind, sensitive, and supportive. Even so, Pema Chodron teaches that we can "aspire" or make the wish to be helpful, planting the seed in our minds and our hearts to act when the time is right.

While we may hope to take on the role of the grandfather and light the way for others right away, it is okay to understand that it takes time and wisdom to know how and when to act. Sometimes, simply cultivating the wholehearted wish to be of service is enough. With patience, we can trust that our aspiration will eventually turn into helpful action when others need us the most. Without judgment, harshness, and at our own pace, we too will be of great benefit as we slowly mature, breathe, and heal along this imperfect path.

CHAPTER 3: OUR BASIC GOODNESS

"I wish I could show you, when you are lonely or in darkness, the astounding light of your own being."

Hafiz

"He who saves a single life, saves the world entire."

The Jewish Talmud

Underneath all the models and identities presented to us in modern-day life, each of us possesses at least a little kindness and understanding for what it means to live somewhere right in the "middle." Right in the middle of inspiration and confusion, wealth and poverty, and pleasure and pain. In her book, *The Places that Scare You: A Guide to Fearlessness in Difficult Times*, Pema Chodron defines this as the "in-between state." Pema Chodron explains that the in-between state is a spiritual spot closer to our basic kindness and compassion. Yet, this is also a place where we still experience our old habitual patterns of fear, harshness, and even anger.

However, sometimes in moments when we are awake and softened by the people and animals around us, our warmth and good spirit can reappear like magic, helping us express our care for others more fully. In

Buddhism, this warmth and care is also known as our "basic goodness," something inherent and untouched despite the inevitable difficulties of being alive at this time and at this moment. Buddhist scholars teach that basic goodness exists in all living beings and that despite our imperfections or mistakes from the past, we are just one mindful breath away from tapping back into that goodness. Even if our fear and confusion has been far greater than our sanity, our fundamental basic goodness remains unscathed and easily reignited through altruism and mindfulness practice.

As we discuss basic goodness and what that might mean to us, I cannot help but think of my father, Mitchell Charles Dorson. For those who did not know him, my father was quite hard of hearing and required a powerful hearing aid to communicate verbally at home and at his job as a teacher. Even so, I still remember him glowing when he saw someone he knew. Whether we were in our hometown of Tucson, Arizona or somewhere more remote, dad would always find a person from his past and strike up a conversation. Free of hesitation, he would run up to a friend or an acquaintance and take delight in their presence. Even if he had seen a particular friend recently, my father would cherish the moment with them as something brand new and enthralling!

His spontaneous joy was so rare it was hard to understand where it came from. It could have been that dad's unique enthusiasm was the result of losing his hearing when he was only five years old from a measles infection. Or my father had steered away from forming and attaching to social cliques because of the wisdom that accompanied his disability. Whatever the reason, dad was fearlessly kind when it came to showing genuine love and care for all people, young and old. Once he made a connection with a person, particularly students that he taught at his high school or in the Jewish community, my father would wrap his arms around them and embrace them as if they were his own child. Those who did not know what to make of him at first would eventually embrace and come to love his infectious spirit and kindness.

This kind of receptiveness and enthusiasm for another person, which my dad actively modeled so well in our home and our community, can alter the direction of a life. I see examples of this all the time when parents hold their children with tenderness after a fall, when teachers work with struggling students and families, or when passerby approach a homeless man, woman, or child on the street to help them find shelter. "What can I do?" and "How may I help?" are lifeline questions, often reminding a child or an adult that they are not alone in their struggles. Reaching out in this way is a gesture of tremendous importance that we should not take lightly.

Throughout my time as an educator and as a member of a Recovery Community, I have witnessed brave and beautiful people listening attentively, withholding judgment, and finding a way to be of service. In these moments, a connection forms between human beings, helping lay the foundation for healing. In most cases, those who wish to help do not know what the next moment will bring despite their best intentions. Even so, extraordinary people all over the country continue to reach out to those in need of guidance, comfort, and support during these immensely confusing times.

However, sometimes we push our kindness and compassion aside to find acceptance and recognition. We want to be genuine, kindhearted, and loyal to the people we love and care for. Still, we desire respect for our own individual qualities. We all know from experience how daunting this juggling act can be, the tightrope of looking out for others while also striving to fulfill our own basic needs.

In my own life, I have tried to resolve walking this narrow road by creating an identity that is lovable and agreeable with the hope of receiving admiration from all sides. In the process of making and re-making this likable image, I relinquished the ability to love and build authentic friendships for a stronger desire to fit in. Of course, at an early age we found a way to blend in. Directly or indirectly, parents and teachers told us not to stand out and become a part of the crowd, even if it meant discounting our own experience and basic intelligence. This is not necessarily a terrible thing, but just the reality.

Going back to grade school, I can still remember craving acceptance from my peers and teachers. I yearned to look thin and have unblemished skin, wear the right clothes, and never say the inappropriate thing at the wrong time. My peers at the "Cool Table" dressed in stylish clothes and displayed an endearing confidence that seemed so alien to me at the time. As I entered high school, I prayed that if I could become part of this crowd, sit with them, and join their world, the growing insecurities of my family and sexual orientation would fade away.

That drive for acceptance and admiration often led me to overlook and end long standing friendships. Unfortunately, I pushed aside faithful friends who had helped me grow and find happiness in the hope of winning favor from those perceived as cool and attractive. As a result, I replaced genuine relationships with the illusion of friendship. Even now I feel anxious and awkward remembering the times when I was so unaware, unkind, and naïve to pursue popularity and praise more than anything else.

While embarrassing and humbling to admit, this struggle to fit in and show genuine kindness compose a core tenet of imperfect healing. Although there may be a tendency to push one of these aspects aside, our exploration begins with experiencing and getting to know both dimensions of ourselves: the things that we consider beautiful and noble and the things that are awkward, embarrassing, and difficult to embrace. We may still long to feel desirable, looking the perfect part. Still, we also could surprise ourselves at times by giving up that desire and finding a way to relate with every person we encounter, free of fear. Even as we read this passage, we may rediscover one hidden part of ourselves bubbling to the surface: vulnerability, the wish to give and show generosity, self-centeredness, the desire to fit in, or the love for another person. Instead of turning away from this experience, we can allow what we feel to help us connect more authentically and consistently with the people in our lives.

Walking this journey together, it is good to remember that everything we encounter, whether it is sweet and pleasant or bitter and embarrassing has a place in our own development. As Pema Chodron teaches in her book, *Start Where You Are: A Guide to Compassionate Living*, all our competing parts make up this indescribable and immeasurable human experience. We can feel like "the world's most hopeless basket-case," she explains, "and still be a good candidate for enlightenment." This teaching touches my heart profoundly and reminds me that our successes and failures, like the tides, eventually come and go. What remains after both have passed is our tender spirit and our ability to witness everything and everyone with equanimity, mindfulness, and even a sense of humor.

From this place of openness and understanding, even for our most challenging human aspects, we can continue the process of learning about imperfect healing through our first meditation together.

Meditation: Relearning Our Basic Goodness

Sensing all parts of your body and mind, breathe in and out. One breath in, one breath out. Two breaths in, two breaths out. Three breaths in, three breaths out. Make this moment as simple as you can by focusing on your breath. Breathe and experience your mind and body in this one place and moment in your life.

Sensing your own desires, longing for connection, allow yourself to relax just where you are. Breathe in and breathe out. Breathe in and breathe out. Feelings or memories may start to come to the surface, bubbling up over time. If this happens, breathe gently, and try to relax just where you are. If a strong sensation, a strong memory, or a strong thought takes hold, bring yourself back to the breath. One breath in, one breath out. Two breaths in, two breaths out. Three breaths in, three breaths out. Just breathe.

Sense deeply what you feel: gratitude, remorse, desire, or expectation. Whatever you experience, see if you can relax any part of your body and mind that is tender, not holding anything back. Let the sensations come and go without struggle. Gently, let the space inside of you keep opening, creating even more room for your experience to find a place to rest. Feel the full weight of your experience for just ten seconds more. 1... 2...3...4...5...6...7...8...9...10.

Gently, in your own time, let whatever you have been holding on to pass away, allowing yourself to come back to your breath. One breath in, one breath out. Two breaths in, two breaths out. Three breaths in, three breaths out.

Gently, return to this moment, opening your eyes if you closed them. If you can, take a moment to take delight in the basic understanding and kindness you have started to develop toward yourself through this practice.

Well done. Well done. Well done.

CHAPTER 4: LOVINGKINDNESS IN EVERYDAY LIFE

**"You belong among the wildflowers...
Far away from your trouble and worry,
You belong somewhere you feel free."**

Tom Petty, *Wildflowers*

As the meditation from the last chapter touches on, each of us has the potential to uncover our basic goodness by being gently mindful of what feels good and pleasant and what does not as we move throughout our days. In the Buddhist tradition, teachers describe this gentle mindfulness as "lovingkindness" or the "practice of lovingkindness." Like the grandfather in the "starfish parable," we too can sense our own innate capacity to show extraordinary love and care for the world even during turbulent times. We nurture and develop this strong capacity to become more loving, kind, and altruistic by incorporating lovingkindness into our daily lives and meditation practice. In her book, *Lovingkindness: The Revolutionary Art of Happiness,* Sharon Salzberg describes lovingkindness as the foundation from which all spiritual life can grow and blossom, helping us cultivate peace and warmth toward ourselves, those closest to us, and even the people we struggle to understand and feel affection for.

There is so much that we wish to communicate to each other. We think and feel so deeply for this world despite the conflict that seems to continue. In these very trying times, it can be difficult to convey our admiration and concern for one another in the speed and anxiety of modern living. Sometimes, we must move with urgency, trying to arrive on time and meet our deadlines promptly. We move so fast in fact that it can be problematic to see the faces of our friends and children waiting beside us at the doctor's office, the coffee shop, or even our loved ones walking through the door at night.

Recently, I remembered this modern-day truth while rushing to breakfast at our extended stay hotel in Denton, Texas. With my hands gripping an iPhone and a notepad stuffed into the crease of my arm, I nearly dropped my plate of eggs and chorizo before a kindly server gently took all my things and placed them on a nearby table. In the voice of love and care she told me, "Folks are always rushing around here. Please, do not rush. I will take five extra minutes to get y'all whatever you need before I clear the food away." This incredibly wise and gentle woman, in response to this constant rushing, taught me what it meant to practice lovingkindness in the moment. By slowing down and putting down anything unnecessary, we can experience our love for the people walking beside us and often helping us throughout the day. Whether it is an iPhone, a notebook, or even something less tangible such as resentment or fear, I understood right then that the practice of lovingkindness was also the practice of letting go and releasing my habitual desire to always be in control.

To begin lovingkindness practice, we can imagine placing our minds in what is known as the "cradle of lovingkindness." This spiritual, physical, and emotional space is one of safety, detached from our daily distractions and worries. Like a child held in their mother's arms for the first time, we can slowly recall the feeling of unconditional love. In a deeply personal way, we rest our minds and bodies with an attitude of tenderness, free of self-judgment. Whether someone is sitting in a meeting with their fellows, walking to work, composing an email, or even brushing their teeth, lovingkindness is always accessible and seeking cultivation.

By practicing lovingkindness, the timidity of making ourselves receptive to the world slowly begins to soften, leaving us gradually in contact with our own wish for intimacy. As Sharon Salzberg explains so beautifully, lovingkindness can serve as a "cohesive factor," a unifying force that brings us together with our own basic goodness and the people we see popping up in our lives year after year. With consistency, this practice has the power to kindle our senses and facilitate the process of making us more present and awake. Lovingkindness can even embolden us to say "hello" to a stranger waiting at the bus stop, look after our neighbors' animals while they are busy at work, or respond patiently to our partner as they talk through a problem of magnitude.

Though we may not know how to express our deepest wish for safety and well-being, both for ourselves and the people we love, I have found the following phrases helpful in developing the practice of lovingkindness:

**"May we be happy and healthy.
May we be joyous and peaceful.
May we be filled with lovingkindness."**

I remember when I first started this practice feeling as though I could only say one phrase before seeing my mind wander off into worry or anxiety. It was frustrating at first trying to cultivate the practice of lovingkindness and not knowing if my mind would accept this style of thinking, let alone being. Even with great ambition and enthusiasm, I was unable to sustain focus for two minutes, let alone the fifteen I had planned for! Without a doubt, it was humbling to witness just how inexperienced and untrained I was at staying present and attentive, even to the most pleasant moments of the day.

In his book, *A Path with Heart: The Perils and Promises of Spiritual Life,* Jack Kornfield describes how our minds can seem like young puppies when we start practicing. At first, our minds move off-balance with the slightest tug, scent, or sensation. Something inevitably catches our eye, and we are off and running headfirst at one-hundred miles per hour. As experience shows, this can happen for an exceptionally long time, even when we are practicing with sincerity. Patiently, Jack Kornfield explains, we can tame our minds by returning to the present moment repeatedly. Moment by moment, we allow our restless minds to tire themselves out in all our old ways of thinking and acting, until we eventually come to a place of rest and wisdom.

Looking back, I remember how important it was for me to practice lovingkindness while training Gizmo when we first got him as a puppy. Initially, he was having a challenging time not destroying his crate in the kitchen and making a complete mess of the house. At that time, I was quite inexperienced and unsure about what to do to help him feel comfortable and safe in his new home. "Should I be sterner and more disciplinary with him? Should I ignore him completely and continue cleaning up the mess? Or should I try to distract him with a new toy, hoping he will wear himself out?" Eventually, I made the decision to carry him upstairs, turn out the lights in the bathroom, and hold him as gently as possible until he settled down and slept in my arms. Although I was not aware of it at the time, I was practicing lovingkindness and patience toward our rambunctious and highly energetic young pup. It did not happen overnight, but through this patient ritual of cradling him, Gizmo would learn to calm down instead of destroying the kitchen.

Like the experience of training Gizmo when he was still young, lovingkindness coupled with patience can tame our minds as well. With practice, lovingkindness can become a stronger force then our old habitual patterns and internal dramas of mind. Letting go of our perception of success and failure, we simply do what we can to compassionately take hold of our minds with wisdom and grace. Finding our breath once more, we return to the moment, relinquishing judgment, or self-criticism if we have become overwhelmed. Eventually, we may even laugh and take delight at witnessing how our minds still desire to make a mess, but like Gizmo, have developed the wisdom to find a nice sunspot to lounge instead of tearing up the carpet.

After about a year of practicing lovingkindness meditation, I found myself repeating each lovingkindness phrase as I walked and prepared for my late-night restaurant shift. Serving burgers and fries, bussing and turning tables, and refilling unending cups of decaf and regular coffee often seemed like a manageable and lighthearted occupation that was in my blood. On other nights however, the stress of cleaning up broken glass, dumping fifteen-pound bags of garbage in a darkened alley, and the restaurant theatrics that I could not avoid made lovingkindness practice an absolute necessity.

Focusing on lovingkindness not only soothed my mind after a long and busy shift, but also on the walk back home at 2:30am on a Sunday morning. Step by step, I would repeat the lovingkindness phrases, taking extra care of my surroundings while enjoying the hum of streetlamps on the quiet city streets. In the crisp night air of the Pacific Northwest, I would pause from time to time and experience a sense of freedom and energy that became stronger with this practice of lovingkindness. That said, catching a cab or an Uber home might be best for people working the late shift and practicing lovingkindness to this same degree.

Years later, my experience bussing tables serves as a valuable teacher. Even if circumstances are not ideal, we can still develop an active mind geared toward mental wellness and self-compassion. While the duties and expectations of service work and making a living will provide various forms of stress, with lovingkindness we can continue to lay the foundation for a joyful life in the future, one that is hopefully a little calmer and with longer breaks!

Inevitably, lovingkindness practice will illuminate both our aspiration to be loving and kind and places where we might feel most stuck and rigid in our thinking. Though this contradiction can be difficult to understand, it points directly to our own process of imperfect healing. As we practice, we begin to understand that fundamental healing will happen in its own time and at its own pace. Thus, we cultivate lovingkindness with the wisdom that we will always be uncovering new dimensions of care and gentleness, hopefully one day modeling for others the benefits this practice may have in their relationships as well.

Through lovingkindness, our challenges and fears may find a way to arise in our consciousness and then pass away. Even when we remember old pain and embarrassment, lovingkindness can serve as an energy source to keep us moving forward, empowering us to connect with fundamental goodness and joy. Over time and with practice, we soften our heaviness of heart and anxiety through lovingkindness, coming back to our own basic strength and innate ability to be kind, compassionate, and loving.

Meditation: Practicing Lovingkindness

Sitting, standing, or even lying down, take a moment to breathe, turning back into your own energy and tenderness. Take five minutes to breathe and feel whatever is happening in your mind and body. Relax your body and remain gently upright, breathing and letting go. Breathe and relax, feeling your breath arise and pass away. Breathe and let go, one moment at a time.

When you sense that you are ready to begin lovingkindness practice, bring the following phrases to mind and start to say them for yourself:

"May I be happy and healthy.
May I be joyous and peaceful.
May I be filled with lovingkindness."

During this initial practice, I often recall a picture of myself as a young boy sitting on our sofa and holding the Jewish Torah Scroll my dad would bring back from our synagogue. In that moment, I remember feeling this tremendous happiness cradling the Torah and wrapping my arms around it until it was time for bed. I could hardly wait to feel its weight and texture on my chest and the tip on my chin. Though I am much, much older now, this picture reminds me of where I started out and how I can bring that same innocence and joy back to life through lovingkindness.

As we practice in this way, thoughts and desires of all kinds may arise, some old and repetitive and some new and surprising. If this happens, remember to breathe, feeling the energy of your discursive thoughts for just for ten more seconds. Then with gentleness, come back to the phrases, reciting them with a bit more steadiness.

Be patient in this practice of devoting lovingkindness toward yourself. Whether you are walking, working, engaging with friends, or even finding time to sit quietly in meditation, bring these phrases to mind in a soft and gentle way:

"May I be happy and healthy.

**May I be joyous and peaceful.
May I be filled with lovingkindness."**

Trust your own pace in this process, remembering that there is nowhere to go at this very moment and nowhere to run off to. Allow your body to breathe as you make your way back to these simple words, letting go of expectation.

Lovingkindness for a Beloved One

If someone comes to mind who you care for, slowly begin to include them in your lovingkindness practice. Sharon Salzberg explains that initially, this person can be someone who has been kind, gentle, and giving toward us in a non-romantic way, if possible. We define this second stage of the practice as sending lovingkindness to our "benefactor" or our "beloved one":

**"May we be happy and healthy.
May we be joyous and peaceful.
May we be filled with loving-kindness."**

Moving into this stage of the practice, I sometimes like to imagine holding hands with the beloved people in my life and forming a circle. This circle, whether we are standing or sitting, serves as an expression of our collective wish to cultivate safety and trust with those we are closest to. In place of fearing that we may cause harm or experience harm, this simple act of taking another person's hands shows our desire to respect, soothe, and even protect the people we cherish in our lives. While we may feel isolated at times and unsure of how to communicate, the image of individuals holding hands can remind us that we have the potential to create an environment that fosters happiness, starting with ourselves and our loved ones.

Lovingkindness for the Neutral Person

Eventually, we may find that our practice can include the people we love and those we have a "neutral" relationship with. In my own daily practice, I have found that sending lovingkindness to people I pass by on the street or at the grocery store is immensely helpful in cultivating a sense of shared connection. While I may not know the people I walk past or see driving by in their cars, I can still connect with their experience of getting up in the morning, preparing for work, and trying to do something positive with their day.

In this third stage of sending lovingkindness to people we consider "neutral" in our lives, we learn further how important it is to walk and talk peacefully with strangers, building the intention to stop causing harm with our bodies, thoughts, and actions. Little by little, through lovingkindness we come to understand that all people share the common bond of experiencing success and failure, pleasure and pain, and joy and sadness. This realization can help us unwind feelings of separateness or loneliness, deepening our commitment to seek out what brings us together rather than what divides and tears us apart.

Lovingkindness for the Enemy

In the fourth stage of the practice, we send lovingkindness to people who may make us uncomfortable or, in more accurate terms, "drive us a little crazy." In the Buddhist tradition, this is also known as sending lovingkindness to the "the enemy." Frankly, it can be daunting to send lovingkindness to a person who makes us uneasy or even afraid. Of course, each of us can think of at least one person or situation that makes us so uncomfortable that we might say internally, "Please, get me the hell out of here!" When such inevitable challenges show up, Sharon Salzberg explains that we can adjust the phrases. Using just a little humor as encouragement, we can say the following:

"Just like me, this person wishes to be happy and healthy. May this person, who is driving me crazy, also be happy and healthy. Just like me, this person wishes to be joyous and peaceful. May this person, who may always drive me crazy, also be joyous and peaceful."

While it may be quite difficult to see our commonality and interconnection with a person we have had conflict with, this shift in our meditation may once more open our eyes to the fact that we are not alone in our experience. All people, regardless of economic background, sexual orientation, ethnicity, race, class, or gender will experience happiness and suffering, and winning and losing. From this point of view, we can learn that our struggles and successes on this planet come from the same stuff and that we are more alike than we could ever imagine.

Lovingkindness for the Whole World

When we feel ready and at our own pace, we can wish lovingkindness to ourselves, the people we love, those we feel neutral toward, and even individuals we dislike in our lovingkindness practice. Arriving at this point in our meditation, we can try to make the practice as wide reaching as possible, reciting our lovingkindness phrases for all people, all over the world, without any conditions or limitations:

"May all of us be happy and healthy.
May all of us be joyous and peaceful.
May all of us be filled with lovingkindness."

If you have been meditating just now, gently come back to your breath and feel the vibration taking place in your body. If the energy you have contacted is intense, see if you can soften and let go, trusting in the tremendous good that this practice will bring about one day. Hold your experience gently, feeling through your mind and body for just ten more seconds. 1...2...3...4... 5...6...7...8...9...10.

When you feel ready, try to let it go, opening your eyes if you have closed them and coming back to this very moment, at your own pace. Let go gently, relaxing back into this one moment filled with lovingkindness.

CHAPTER 5: WARRIOR SLOGANS IN CHALLENGING TIMES

"I learned that courage was not the absence of fear, but the triumph over it. The brave man is not he who does not feel afraid, but he who conquers that fear."
Nelson Mandela

On a deeply personal level, my own experience with imperfect healing has often been one of attempting to ride the difficulties of spiritual and daily life. As we discussed in earlier chapters, learning to ride these waves has often meant exploring the sheer power of emotions and events with a little more care and wisdom, even when something unexpectedly happens. Although we may lose our cool and get upset at times in this unpredictable journey, we have also benefitted from learning how to fall and pick ourselves back up a little quicker as the years progress. Although we may never get it quite right and be perfect spiritual practitioners, there is joy in the process of trying, stumbling, falling, and getting back up again.

Sometimes, our lives have a grounded quality, a strength and happiness that is durable and able to embrace whatever comes our way. When we are fortunate enough to experience such happiness, our minds and bodies can suddenly let go and remember the newness and freshness of the world. We see this type of wonder all the time when children frolic and allow themselves to savor every note and tenure of their youthful happiness. When we are fortunate to witness such carefree exuberance, our hearts can find a way back to our own childlike spirit and abiding love for the world.

I remember such a time when I first moved in with Zim. Although we had been friends for quite a while, something about living with each other felt different, but also safe and comfortable. In our small apartment and neighborhood, we would spend time eating meals with each other, going on walks in the mornings and evenings, and watching our favorite shows on television during the weekends such as *Downtown Abbey*, *The West Wing*, and *Six Feet Under*. Zim soothed my anxiety through his kind and constant way of being, despite my fear of falling in love with a man. Up until that point, I had never allowed myself to feel such a connection with any person. After more than ten years of companionship, I still cherish our time together, understanding with age and experience just how precious our relationship is.

Yet, about a year into our courtship my father, who had been struggling with acute physical and emotional pain, committed suicide. Years after the fact, it is impossible to express the full depth and impact of his passing. My dad was my best friend and my lifelong protector. He had held me in lovingkindness during my darkest moments and with great care, had seen me through to better days filled with stability, love, and hope.

Without Zim walking beside me, I am not sure I would have been able to pack and dress myself to make the trip home to commemorate his life. On the days leading up to funeral, I could barely see beyond the continuous sting of tears flowing out me in private and public. I remember going with Zim to a department store in Seattle to buy slacks and a shirt for the memorial in Tucson in less than a week. When we closed the doors to the changing room, the tears started all over again, making my face look almost unrecognizable. My heart, visibly broken, grieved openly and without shame of being noticed or even seen by strangers.

During this very painful time, my whole being, experiencing bolts of confusion and trauma, searched for the right words to express and soothe this pain. I remember coming home from work at my restaurant job shortly after his passing and sitting in the lobby of our apartment building throughout the early morning. I still remember the sensations of being numb, confused, and frightened. It was such an emotional time with the adrenaline pumping through my veins like liquid fire, leaving me often crying or unsure of what to do next. I will never forget sitting in a lounge chair of the lobby, listening to the hum of the Coca-Cola Soda Machine, and experiencing every emotion and sensation imaginable.

Losing my dad was a jolt to my system that made simple activities like walking, brushing my teeth, and even tying my shoes a challenge. That place inside of me nurtured by his paternal care now seemed empty and wounded. The vulnerability of not being mature or strong enough to manage such an immense loss left my body timid and weak. My shoulders and stomach were not in decent shape, to say the least. It is something amazing and frightening to witness how the body changes and reacts when placed under acute stress and I wondered, "How much longer can this go on for?"

It was around this time that I really dove into lovingkindness practice and started composing personal slogans to help my mind and body stay grounded in the present. Finding just a little space from dad's funeral, I recalled Jack Kornfield's meditation on compassion and how to mindfully experience pain during times of profound suffering. Jack Kornfield's description of pain as a fire and a tool that could burn through us as a means of transformation and healing, resonated deeply within me. Sitting in the early morning while it was still dark, trying to compose myself, I started to formulate short mantras to help me experience the pain of dad's death mindfully, letting my fears unravel and unbind themselves in a safe place. Breathing in and out, I started repeating the following slogan to myself:

"May this pain heal in its own time. May this pain heal in its own time. May this pain (please) heal in its own time."

While I wanted to run, disappear, and change my face to become someone else for a little while, I knew that I could not ignore the complexity of emotions that were quickly coming to the surface. I needed an anchor that resonated in my heart to keep my mind and body active and moving forward. Coming back to this mantra and others in times of comfort and in times of fear served as a daily tonic like the altruism of my fellows in recovery.

I would continue to develop compassionate slogans while sitting in support groups and recovery meetings, finding the rhythm of the words soothing to my still mixed up and tender mind. It was comforting to know that a growing number of "warrior slogans," as Pema Chodron calls them, were right at my fingertips, each one acting as a balm for my wounds. Whenever a spare moment appeared for practice, whether I was alone or in a meeting, I would repeat one of my mantras and allow it to carry me a little further along the way into a deeper experience of imperfect healing.

Since that time, I have continued composing mantras or short slogans to sooth the root of this pain and loss. My personal slogans, like the ones practiced in Pema Chodron's *Start Where You Are: A Guide to Compassionate Living,* demonstrate our capacity to open and move forward, despite our wounds. As Pema Chodron explains, we can instruct ourselves in the "dharma" or truth by developing a spiritual vocabulary all our own. With time, practice, and patience, our own warrior slogans can start to interrupt the cyclical pattern of discursive and even harmful thoughts. We may even find through this practice a deeper internal healing for our most hidden pieces and a shift in how we meet struggle and adversity.

Looking at the daily news, it is easy to believe that human beings are fundamentally flawed and beyond redemption. We can so easily make ourselves and others into caricatures and villains, stripping away any semblance of humanity or good will. It is such a sad thing to see how we tear each other down because of confusion and fear based on ideology and antiquated concepts of needing to make ourselves right and someone else wrong. In our current political and cultural landscape, it is much more challenging to see the good in someone and much easier to focus our energy on what we dislike and even hate.

However, warrior slogans that come from deep within have the power to shift our perspective and bring us back to our basic care and faith in each other. Inevitably, challenging times between people will arise, sometimes unexpectedly. Even so, by developing our own warrior slogans, we can find a way to remain upright and sensitive to each other. At a most basic level, we can find a way to still care, even when times get uncomfortable and we want to turn angry, mean, and aggressive.

I often find myself reciting personal slogans during all kinds of emotional storms with friends, family, at work, and at home. My own warrior slogans look something like this:

"May we look upon each other with kindness and safety once more."

"May fear, anxiety, and harm be healed."

"May I see the good in myself and allow it to grow with time."

Each warrior slogan, while slightly different, conveys a personal aspiration for awakening and becoming more sensitive and gentler. With practice, these mantras may help us reach toward a profound transformation, sparking a renewed connection with the world that is more peaceful and safer than before. The work of finding the right phrase or phrases that express our most sincere understanding takes time and patience. If we are lucky enough to create space from the busyness of the daily grind, we may begin to hear our own authentic voice, a voice that shows us what we feel most deeply and what we know inherently to be true.

Using what we have read and learned thus far, we can use this next meditation to cultivate our own mantras or warrior slogans, drawing upon our wisdom to facilitate healing, both in body and mind.

Meditation: Taking Time to Hear Our Own Compassionate Voice

When the time presents itself, even if it is just a half an hour, find a comfortable place to sit and notice your breath. Like before, feel the breath coming in and going out. One breath in, one breath out. Two breaths in, two breaths out. Three breaths in, three breaths out.

After five to ten minutes of mindful breathing, see if you can hear your own strength and goodness speaking through you. What do you wish most for yourself and your loved ones? What words could you think or speak that may help you and the community heal in time? What do you know in your heart to be true?

Take time with these questions and see what arises. Give your own voice time and space to emerge when it is ready. If words come to mind that could be a mantra or a slogan, see how they affect your mind and body. Are your words soothing and kind? Do they loosen and heal any tension within?

As if you were molding clay, work with your slogan. If it is a good fit, write it down and reflect on it throughout the day, noticing if you feel a change or a shift in your mind and body. If difficult feelings or memories arise in response to your mantra, just as in lovingkindness practice, be patient and give yourself time. Simply be with your own words, trusting that they hold an enormous potential for your own health and well-being.

Gently, come back to your own breath, letting go of your slogan or mantra and trusting that it will return at the right time. Come back to your breath and relax, feeling the in and out from your body once more.

Meditation: Forgiving Each Other and Ourselves

Starting again, breathe gently into your body.

Breathing in, breathing out. Breathing in, breathing out. See if you can relax and soften any stiffness that you may feel deep in your mind and body. With a kind touch, allow any discomfort to take shelter in your steady breath. One breath in, one breath out. One breath in, one breath out. One breath in, one breath out. Gently, tenderly, soften your whole being, feeling through parts both tender and strong. Breathe in, breathe out. Breathe in, breathe out. Breathe in, breathe out.

When you feel ready, recall a person you wish to ask forgiveness from. This person may be someone you know quite well presently or someone from the past. Gently, bring this person to mind, seeing their eyes and seeing their face. Sensing any harm, fear, or even abandonment you may have caused, *intentionally or unintentionally,* bring this person into your heart gently *breathing in* their fears or wounds from the past. On the *out-breath*, *breathe out* and *send out* to this individual a sincere and compassionate healing. Breathe out a light tenderness that soothes their worries and fears, slowly beginning the process of mending what may still need time to heal.

As your connection to this process deepens, bring the following phrases to mind, directing these words to the person you are asking forgiveness from:

"May I please be forgiven for any harm, intentional or unintentional, that I have caused you."

"May you please accept my heartfelt apology."

Let the vulnerability of this moment deepen the well of healing making its way to the surface. If you can, bring your breath to these words of forgiveness, sending out an even deeper longing for healing and reconciliation. Breathe and give the process of forgiveness time to unravel at its own pace. Breathe, forgive, and let go. Breathe, forgive, and let go. Breathe, forgive, and let go.

Breathing and feeling through the sensations coming out of your mind and body, send that same quality and forgiveness of healing to yourself, using the following phrases to begin the process of mending your own pain and suffering from the past:

"May I please be forgiven for any harm, intentional or unintentional, that I have caused myself."

"May I please accept this heartfelt forgiveness."

Gently, courageously, see if you can accept this deep forgiveness for yourself. Allow it to touch all your wounds long held within your body, relieving any lingering guilt or shame. Seeing your own tender heart and your own deep longing to let go of harm, give yourself permission to forgive and begin again from a place of safety, peace, and trust. Breathe and feel this process unwinding and healing, both for yourself and the person you seek forgiveness from.

Gently, let go into a space of harmlessness, releasing the past and coming back into the present moment. Breathe once more, in and out, honoring this courageous work and trusting in your own noble heart, once more.

CHAPTER 6–WORKING WITH SOCIAL ANXIETY AND PRACTICING TONGLEN

"I do a visualization: I send my positive emotions like happiness and affection to others. Then another visualization. I visualize receiving their sufferings, their negative emotions. I do this every day."
His Holiness the Dalai Lama, *The Wisdom of Forgiveness*

Like so many of us out there, I too have struggled with social anxiety and relaxing during coffee get-togethers, brunching with friends, and even celebrations over games and movies. Approaching the beautiful middle age of forty, I still find it challenging to not take myself so seriously during moments of celebration and frivolity! In these confusing times throughout the country, it might be a good question to ask, "Why does it have to be so complicated to take delight in the company of people that I love spending time with?"

Even eye contact, something so basic and necessary for our well-being, can seem too intimate when I am having a one-on-one conversation. While talking with a close friend or a person in recovery, it can feel like an obstacle course just to know how and when to look into another person's eyes. "Should I look *now*, or should I look away? How long should I gaze without seeming completely odd and eccentric?" Although humorous and embarrassing to admit, this is the content of my mind that shows up at every party, Bar and Bat Mitzvah, and formal dinner since I was thirteen years old!

Making friends with these old fears of looking foolish and wearing emotions on my sleeve has been a big part of my own imperfect healing. Consequently, when social anxiety does creep up and begin to take a stronger hold, it is becoming my practice to stop and consciously breathe. If I can find a moment to step back from a group or conversation, I try to tell myself internally or out loud, "Just breathe, Noah. Just breathe."

At first, when I remember to do this I experience a tightening or burning in my shoulders or stomach. While I know that this is where I hold anxiety in my body, it is amazing that I am always surprised when it arises again. Little by little, I work to meet these difficult sensations with tenderness, *breathing into* the knots of tension that have reappeared and seeing if they can soften and fade away with time. If I can calm down and even close my eyes for ten more seconds, on the next *out-breath* I image *sending out* a soothing touch to soften the physical stiffness of my body. Likewise, if this breathing practice has brought up not only physical sensations, but also emotions like fear or shame, on the *out-breath* I *send out* kindness, self-compassion, and the wish to start again with a clearer perspective.

This exercise of *breathing into* what is uncomfortable and *breathing out* what is healing and soothing, is an ancient Tibetan practice known as tonglen. Tonglen is a Tibetan meditation technique that means "sending and receiving." Tonglen can be a powerful tool for our purpose of imperfect healing because, like lovingkindness, it is available at any time. Pema Chodron explains that we do not need a huge catastrophe in our lives to begin practicing tonglen. On the contrary, we can start with ourselves and the small difficulties or imperfections we encounter every day. Whether it is a toothache, an unexpected bill, or even restlessness for a job interview, Pema Chodron teaches that we can "drop the story line," the thoughts running through our head and *breathe into* the sensations churning up behind those thoughts. Without blocking or placing extreme judgments on ourselves, we can feel our experience deeply, whether it is joyful or upsetting. Then, on the *out-breath* we let go of whatever we are holding on to and *send out* the best medicine of our own hearts. In this way, we have the chance to unblock our discomfort or excitement and use it as energy to relax, soften, and begin again.

Tonglen is a wonderful and effective practice for allowing all parts of ourselves to arise compassionately and then pass away with less and less resistance over time. Instead of moving away from who we are or what we feel, we practice "leaning into" our thoughts and emotions, getting to know what is underneath this deep-seated longing to pull away. When we are at a party and suddenly feel like the strange quack because we said something odd or inappropriate, we can practice *breathing into* the immediate experience of vulnerability and embarrassment. Then, on the next *out-breathe*, we can *send out* any strength we may need to relax, laugh at ourselves, and then continue. When we are at a meeting, walking down an unknown street, or unsure of how to talk to someone we care for, we can allow everything we feel to make us more tender and help us continue along this path of healing.

The dynamic thing about tonglen is that it is not just for moments when we feel unwell or anxious, but also when we are experiencing good moments of health and well-being. In the same spirit as before, we *breathe into* our happiness, feeling that exuberance and childlike quality throughout our whole being, getting to know what those sensations feel like as well. Then, on the next *out breath,* we *send out* those positive vibrations to everyone we hold dear, wishing that they too may share in our health, renewed sense of potential, and our relative peace and safety.

Indeed, the practice is twofold, allowing us to transform any energy, whether it is positive or negative, into the medicine of imperfect healing. With time and patience, we can meet our feelings of uneasiness, longing, and even excitement with a more mindful approach. Over time, tonglen may sooth our habit of becoming overwhelmed at social events until the practice becomes like second nature, allowing us to relax increasingly with whatever comes next.

Meditation—Tonglen, Sending and Receiving Healing

Gently, allow your body to take in oxygen without struggle. Without hurrying or rushing away, feel the breath enter your body. As naturally as possible, allow the breath to *come in* and then *release* from your body at its own pace. One breath in, one breath out. Two breaths in, two breaths out. Three breaths in, three breaths out. Taking your time, practice simply feeling the breath come in and out of your body. Take your time and go at your own pace, just breathing.

If any feelings or sensations arise, whether they are pleasant or uncomfortable, see if you can continue breathing, feeling that energy. If you can, relax a little more with each breath. One breath in, one breath out. Two breathes in, two breathes out. Then, on the next *out-breath,* see if you can *send out* something soothing. It can be a light breeze, a memory, a kind embrace, or anything that brings you peace. Allow the breath to come in and gently leave, taking with it just a piece of the goodness and compassion that you hold inside your heart. Patiently, keep working with this practice, *breathing into* your own energy, and *sending out* your own beauty and well-being.

As you continue to breathe in, see if you can feel the energy of your mind and body a little deeper and relax a little further. Let whatever arises soften your mind, relaxing any tension that remains in your body. Once more, try to meet your memories, feelings, and thoughts with a steady breath, a breath that may open to anything. Gently, on the *out-breath*, try to *send out* just a little bit more healing, both for yourself and others close to your heart. Send this healing to anyone you feel love and genuine care for: your spouse, children, friends, neighbors, or even the people you consider kind acquaintances on the street. Keep *sending out* your own soothing and compassionate heart until you can feel it reaching wider and wider beyond your own body.

When you feel ready, come back to just focusing on your breath, the gentle in and out. Just come back to yourself, relaxing and letting go, just breathing.

At any point in the day, whether we are feeling healthy and strong or frustrated and unsure, we can remember that the practice of tonglen is available to us. We can remember that with this training we can learn to *breathe into* our immediate experience and *breathe out*, the best and most gentle of what is inside of our hearts.

Patiently and with kindness, keep breathing and relaxing until you feel able to move forward into the next moment of the day, just a little more at peace and in touch with your own compassionate heart.

CHAPTER 7: SEEING A LITTLE MORE CLEARLY THE PRECIOUSNESS OF LIFE

"For life is holy and every moment is precious."
Jack Kerouac

As we engage more with our own path, feeling through the desires and joys that accompany us wherever we go, we may witness the ongoing process of change happening within and all around us. Whether we are switching jobs, moving to a new place, or entering a new relationship, our experience can suddenly appear as fluid as water running down a rocky brook. Even our bodies with every breath mold, reform, mold, and reform from one moment to the next.

We know how humbling it can be at times to see ourselves in this process of change and adaptation. However, as we make our way down this imperfect spiritual road, we can slowly acknowledge that our time on this planet is fleeting, impermanent, and precious. When we lose someone we love, this impermanence amplifies the preciousness of life and teaches us to savior and cherish what we have, right here and right now. While we may not always get what we want or get what we want after the desire has passed, there is always a chance to experience the tremendous ebb and flow of life. Like a leaf floating down a stream finding its way through the unknown waters, we too can cultivate that same equanimity to experience every nuisance of this precious existence, even when we are humbled and unsure of what to do next.

We find this sacred expression of what it means to live fully despite uncertainty in the poetry of an anonymous southern soldier during the American Civil War. In his own spiritual prose, he writes:

"I asked God for strength, that I might achieve;
I was made weak, that I might learn humbly to obey.
I asked for health, that I might do greater things;
I was given infirmity, that I might do better things.
I asked for riches, that I might be happy;
I was given poverty, that I might be wise.
I asked for power, that I might have the praise of men;
I was given weakness, that I might feel the need of God.
I asked for all things, that I might enjoy life;
I was given life, that I might enjoy all things.
I got nothing that I asked for, but everything I hoped for.
Almost despite myself, my unspoken prayers were answered.
I am among all men most richly blessed."

This was one of my father's most treasured poems, one which he would recite from memory to our family and his students as often as possible. This poem exemplified my dad's life and how he tried to live from a place of sacredness and acceptance in the face of great personal challenges. Through sickness and health, in good times and not such good times, my father would find a connection to the world and the people of it that went beyond his own physical limitations and even his sorrow. No matter what happened to him or how ill he became near the end, he strove to cultivate gentleness, humility, and wisdom. Like the brave soldier in the poem, he too aspired to see good in the world and find its beauty until the day he died.

Through our own awareness and our ability to endure and live fully, we can take the next step and stop fighting life. In place of struggle, we can work with our emotions and anxieties, relearning to walk, swim, write, and breathe with our feelings just as they come. No doubt, it takes time to cultivate such a courageous attitude, like that of the soldier and my dear dad. It can take years, if not a whole lifetime, to look at the world and ourselves with such openness and genuine compassion. However, the more we stop and breathe, feeling the movement of our heart, the depth of body and mind, vivid and unknowable, we can begin to relax with being right in the middle, trusting that we have what it takes to be present and awake in this very instant, in this precious moment.

Meditation: Seeing Ourselves a Little More Clearly

Take time to find space for yourself. This space you are providing is precious, sacred, and life-affirming. This space is a necessary gift, one that would benefit all people. For just a moment, take a beat to gently acknowledge that this is good! Providing yourself time to be mindful is a wonderful gift that will help create the conditions for healing and for sustaining joy.

Breathe in, sensing any sensation that might be present in your body. Even with sustained practice, we will eventually encounter discomfort. If discomfort is present, simply acknowledge it and on the out-breath see if you can soften and let go. Each of us possesses a depth of wisdom, understanding, and connection with the world. As we move along this path, we may find this wisdom growing stronger, just a little more every day.

If a flash of understanding and connection arises, see if you can say aloud, "Ah, I see. I see." Let these connections remind you of your own inherent strength and wisdom. "Ah, I see, I see." With steadiness, feel the breath rise and fall, seeing your mind, body, and heart with a little more clarity, openness, and acceptance: "Ah, I see, I see." Breathe, open, and let go. Breathe, open, and let go. Breathe, open, and let go.

Slowly, coming back to this one moment, breathe in and out, opening a little further and letting go once more.

CHAPTER 8: ENDING WITH GRATITUDE

"Gratitude, like faith, is a muscle. The more you use it, the stronger it grows."
Alan Cohen

It is 7:04pm on Monday in Denton, Texas and I am ready to give Gizmo his dinner, last walk of the night, and finally prepare TV microwaveable meals with Zim when he returns home from work. Given the unforeseeable things that could go wrong over twenty-four hours, I cannot help but feel relief wash over me when he walks through the door and the three of us are together again. We may not be the typical American family, but there is still quite a bit of love, tenderness, and playfulness in our one-bedroom suite.

We are still at our extended stay hotel and still relying on the microwave to provide nutrition meals at a reasonable price. While people may give extended stay hotels and motels a bad rap after staying awhile, I love it here! I love the people who run the front desk and keep the coffee and cookies rolling in. I love the engineers who take care of the swimming pool and work without complaint so that youngsters have a chance to play and stay cool in the summer. I love the service staff that make breakfast for us every morning and often wait an extra ten minutes before taking the food away when I am running behind schedule. I love the ladies who clean our hotel room and tease me about how I try and fail to speak Spanish to them. They are so kind and considerate, making this place feel like a home away from home, even when they are off the clock. And of course, I love my fellow guests who have shared their lives, wisdom, and Rummikub Boards with us. After five weeks in Denton, Texas, it is amazing to reflect that every person we have formed relationships with has been kind and understanding, not only to Zim and me, but also to Gizmo when he is acting crazy and rambunctious.

If I were to be completely honest, this book could not have been possible without the daily sacrifices completed on our behalf. Without the gentle conversation, laughter, delicious food, and patience in response to my constant demands on their business center and printer, I do not know what I would do. Thus, I am beyond grateful! I am grateful for the people in my life that I have just met and will hopefully stay connected with when we eventually leave here. I am grateful for having the comfort, safety, and time to write my first book, green and inexperienced as I may be. And I am also grateful that we have had the chance to come here and see a new place, with fresh faces and destinations awaiting us in the future.

While I am currently unemployed and do not have the security of a 9-5, the diligent practice of writing every day has graced my mind and body with inspiration, intense feelings of delight, and even the endurance to finish! This daily focus of reading, writing, and editing, although maddening at times, has also lifted my spirits. Like lifting weights, the practice of composing *Imperfect Healing* has given me quite a workout. While fatigued and a bit frightened that no one will buy this book, let alone read it, I still feel at peace. I feel at peace knowing that I have done my absolute best that I could do, and I am ready to send it out there into the world.

For everyone who has read these chapters and had the patience to complete the book, I cannot thank you enough for taking the time to walk with me down this imperfect road drafted with an imperfect style and flair all my own. It remains one of my deepest aspirations that this book, in a minute way, may be a pebble of support in your own journey, one filled with some hills, plateaus, but also many, many wonderful experiences along the way.

With all my heart, I love you and hope you take wonderful care!

Meditation: Healing as We Sleep and Starting Again

As you fall asleep, remembering all the courageous work you have undertaken in your practice so far, may you relax and allow your body to find a deep place of rest and healing. Breathing in, and breathing out. Breathing in, and breathing out. Breathing in, and breathing out. If you are holding any discomfort or tension, let your breath touch those places, helping them unwind and release.

Breath by breath, sensation by sensation, may you find safe shelter and peace as you allow yourself space from the daylight hours of work. Breathing in, and breathing out. Breathing in and breathing out. Breathing in, and breathing out. May you peacefully fall asleep, letting go till you awake in the morning.

NOAH MICAH DORSON

REFERENCES:

Quotes:

Shantideva. *"If with mindfullness' rope, the elephant of the mind is tethered all around, our fears will come to nothing, every virtue drop into our hands."* Excerpt from *No Time to Lose: A Timely Guide to The Way of the Bodhisattva*. Chodron, Pema. (2005).

A Beginning: King, Martin Luther King, Jr. *"We must accept finite disappointment, but never lose infinite hope."* https://parade.com/252644/viannguyen/15-of-martin-luther-king-jr-s-most-inspiring-motivational-quotes/. (2022).

Chapter 1: Roshi, Suzuki. *"Each of you is perfect the way you are...and you could use a little improvement!"* https://quotecatalog.com/quote/suzuki-roshi-each-of-you-is-Ra3M5b7/.

Chapter 2: Neibuhr, Reinhold. *"God, grant me the serenity to the accept the things I cannot change, courage to change the things I can, and the wisdom to know the difference."* https://www.celebraterecovery.com/resources/cr-tools/serenityprayer.

Chapter 3: Hafiz. *"I wish I could show you, when you are lonely or in darkness, the astounding light of your own being."* https://www.speakingtree.in/allslides/the-happiness-mantra/150514.

Chapter 3. The Talmud. *"He who saves a single life, saves the world entire."* https://

jewinthecity.com/2013/09/he-who-saves-just-one-life-saves-the-world-entire/. (2013).

Chapter 4: Petty, Tom. *"You belong among the wildflowers...Far away from your trouble and worry,You belong somewhere you feel free."* https://genius.com/Tom-petty-wildflowers-lyrics.

Chapter 5: Mandela, Nelson. *"I learned that courage was not the absence of fear, but the triumph over it. The brave man is not he who does not feel afraid, but he who conquers that fear."* https://borgenproject.org/nelson-mandelas-quotes-on-fear/.

Chapter 6: HHS The Dalai Lama. *"I do a visualization: I send my positive emotions like happiness and affection to others. Then another visualization. I visualize receiving their sufferings, their negative emotions. I do this every day."* Excerpt from *The Wisdom of Forgiveness: Intimate Conversations and Journeys* (see "Book Resources" below).

Chapter 7: Kerouac, Jack. *"For life is holy and every moment is precious."* https://www.internetpillar.com/life-is-precious-quotes/.

Chapter 7. Anonymous. *"I asked God for strength, that I might achieve; I was made weak, that I might learn humbly to obey. I asked for health, that I might do greater things; I was given infirmity, that I might do better things. I asked for riches, that I might be happy; I was given poverty, that I might be wise.*

I asked for power, that I might have the praise of men;
I was given weakness, that I might feel the need of God.
I asked for all things, that I might enjoy life;
I was given life, that I might enjoy all things.
I got nothing that I asked for, but everything I hoped for. Almost despite myself, my unspoken prayers were answered. I am among all men most richly blessed." https://www.myincrediblewebsite.com/i-asked-god-for-strength-poem-and-prayer/.

Chapter 8: Cohen, Alan. *"Gratitude, like faith, is a muscle. The more you use it, the stronger it grows."* https://www.overallmotivation.com/quotes/alan-cohen-quotes/.

Book Resources:

1. Chan, Victor, and HHS The Dalai Lama. *The Wisdom of Forgiveness: Intimate Conversations and Journeys.* Penguin Group (USA) Inc (2004). New York.
2. Chodron, Pema. *Start Where You Are: A Guide to Compassionate Living.* Shambhala Publications, Inc (2003). Boston, Massachusetts.
3. *When Things Fall Apart: Heart Advice for Difficult Times.* Shambhala Publications, Inc (2016). Boulder, Colorado.
4. *The Places That Scare You: A Guide to Fearlessness in Difficult Times.* Shambhala Publications, Inc (2002). Boulder, Colorado.
5. Kornfield, Jack. *A Path with Heart: The Perils and Promises of Spiritual Life.* Bantam Publications (1993). New York.
6. Salzberg, Sharon. *Lovingkindness: The Revolutionary Art of Happiness.* Shambhala Publications, Inc (1995). Boulder, Colorado.

Buddhist Meditation Peer Recovery Group Meeting Guide/Script

(Buddha statue and meditation bell are set up in the most accessible location for the group, along with a donation basket.)

Good (morning/evening) and welcome to Buddhist Meditation Peer Recovery. My name is _____ and I will be facilitating (today's/tonight's) group. We come together to practice meditation and study the Buddhist path to awaken, heal, and let go of any unhelpful or compulsive behaviors.

We welcome all who wish to incorporate meditation and Dharma, also known as truth, into their path. People of all faiths, atheist, and agnostic are welcome to this group, coming together with the primary purpose of healing. In this space, we are friends on the road of recovery. Please ask for resources of other groups and programs of recovery after the meeting if you wish. We are here to support each other in fellowship and trust.

Group Guidelines
While participating in group, we observe the following guidelines to promote trust and confidentiality:

1. Please arrive in a substance free state, open to the Dharma and fully able to participate.

2. Be aware of the size of the group when speaking, to allow all who desire a chance to share—**3 to 4 minutes per-check-in if possible.**

3. Maintain confidentiality at all times. Who you see here and what you hear here, stays here.

4. We are a peer support group, not a therapy group. Please use "I Statements" and draw from your own experience when sharing.

5. Please arrive on-time, end on time, and silence all devices (*meeting times are listed at the top.*)

Check-In:
We will begin our meeting with a brief check-in, going around the circle. Check-in is a good time to introduce ourselves, share how our week has been, and what our intention may be for the meditation. Please do not feel any pressure to share if you do not feel like doing so today. First name introductions are just fine. Anyone can begin. (*pause and wait.*) …My name is _____.

(*People in the circle share their first name and do a check in if they wish.*)

Reading:
(*Facilitator introduces and reads the first part of a Dharma passage. **Please pass around the text so that each member of the group has a chance to read and join in. 5-10 minutes if possible**)*

Meditation:
We will now practice meditation for 20 minutes. I will lead the first part of our sit in a guided meditation. After the meditation, we will have a short break, followed by a checkout about our experience and how we are doing.

One bell ring (*ring bell once*) will indicate beginning. Three rings will signal the end of the meditation. Are there any questions before we begin?

(*Take a moment...**One Bell Ring.***)

Guided Meditation:
(*Take a moment to pause and make sure everyone is settling down for the meditation. Check in with yourself as well.*)

As we breathe in...may we please grant ourselves the opportunity to breathe out gently. One in...one out. Two in...two out. Three in... three out...

In the rush of daily life, it is so easy to lose track of our breathing. This morning/evening, as much as we can, may we rest our attention in the basic sensations of breathing. In...and out.

This practice is very old... and we are part of a long lineage of people who have practiced being kind and compassionate to ourselves and to each other...With this in mind, may we be mindful and kind, compassionate, and even joyful to whatever arises during meditation...

Our bodies and minds are designed to feel, to think, to sense, to dream, to imagine, and to care for. If a feeling comes up... hot or cold... feelings of well-being or hunger, pleasant, painful, or neutral sensations, may we try to greet them with an easy and soft touch with the breath...

If thoughts arise at the door step of our mind, may we try to see them just as thoughts and let them go... If we feel comfortable, we can try labeling our thoughts as "thinking, thinking" and gently return to the in-and-out of the breath...

With time and practice, may we trust that our ability to feel and relax will grow...May we trust that we will develop the ability to grow stronger and heal, a little bit at a time.

Silent Meditation
(*We sit silently for the remaining minutes leading to 20 minutes.*)

(*Three Bell Rings*)

Please take your time to come back into full awareness of the space. Please go slow and take your time.

Short Break
We now have time to take a short break. Please feel free to get coffee or tea, stretch, use the restroom, or simply chat with other folks before our last segment of the meeting. Let's meet back in about 5 minutes.

Checkout

We now come to our check-out part of our meeting. Please feel free to share your experience of the reading and meditation and what may have resonated with you today. (*Check-out should come to an end 5 minutes or so before the end of the meeting time.*)

Announcements

Does anyone have any announcements for the good of the group?

(*Now is a good time to make sure folks are informed about Northwest Buddhist Recovery, other Recovery Groups, and upcoming events at SASG or elsewhere.*)

Sharing of Merit and Closing

Our last practice together before closing is the practice of offering Mettā or Lovingkindness. Meditating and sharing together, we may have accumulated positive energy or good karma. Instead of holding this merit to ourselves, we practice sharing it with all beings. Here are some words that can help us to freely offer this goodness. You may say them silently or repeat them aloud if you like.

(Please ask the group if they could stand and hold hands before the final meditation)

(*Pause after each line so the group can respond.*)

May I be happy and healthy.

May I be joyous and peaceful.

May I be filled with Loving-kindness.

May I be freed from suffering.

May we be happy and healthy.
May we be joyous and peaceful.
May we be filled with Loving-kindness.
May we be freed from suffering.

May all beings be happy and healthy.
May all beings be joyous and peaceful.
May all beings be filled with Loving-kindness.
May all beings be freed from suffering.

(Meeting is now concluded.)

Note: Business meetings will be held at the ***beginning of each month***. Please end the meeting on these occasions 5-10 minutes early to discuss ideas, issues, and opportunities for training that participants can utilize. Best of Luck!

NOAH MICAH DORSON

About the Author:

Noah Dorson received his Master's in Teaching from City University in 2013 and worked with students at the middle school level for the next eight years. During that time, he was active in Communities of Recovery in the Seattle area, attending and facilitating Peer Recovery Meditation and Support Groups. Noah currently lives in North Central Texas with his partner, Zim, and dog, Gizmo. *Imperfect Healing: A Meditation on Beginning Again in America* is his first book.

Made in the USA
Las Vegas, NV
23 July 2022

52061703R00049